POSY EDWARDS

ZAC efron
yearbook 2010

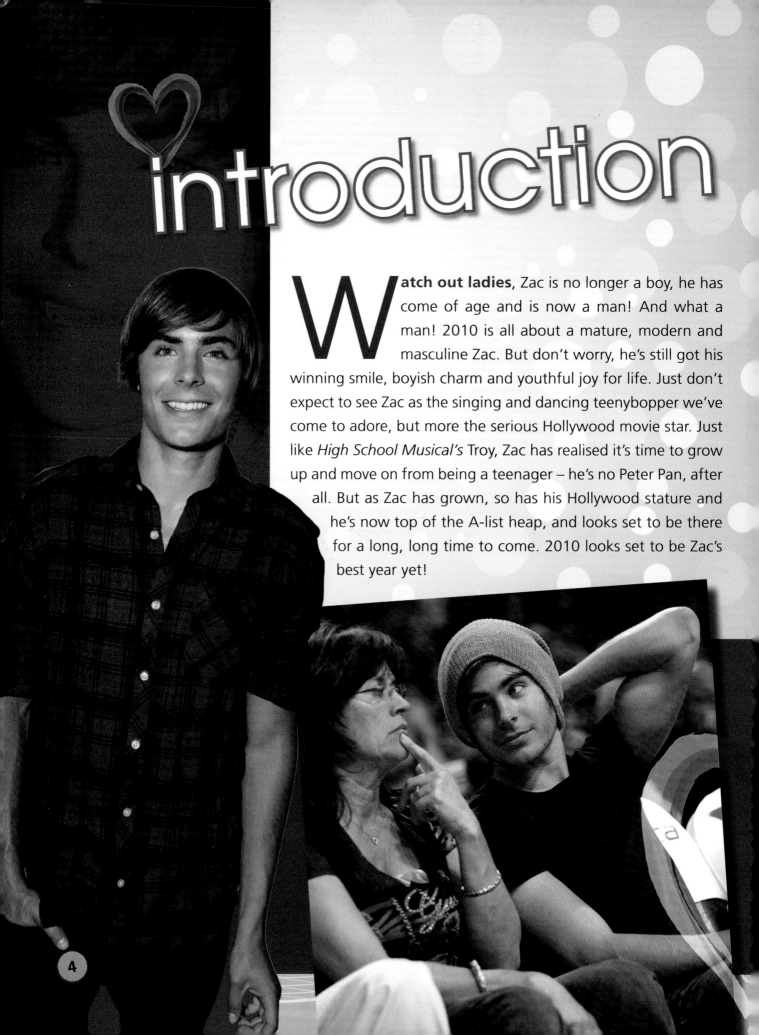

introduction

Watch out ladies, Zac is no longer a boy, he has come of age and is now a man! And what a man! 2010 is all about a mature, modern and masculine Zac. But don't worry, he's still got his winning smile, boyish charm and youthful joy for life. Just don't expect to see Zac as the singing and dancing teenybopper we've come to adore, but more the serious Hollywood movie star. Just like *High School Musical's* Troy, Zac has realised it's time to grow up and move on from being a teenager – he's no Peter Pan, after all. But as Zac has grown, so has his Hollywood stature and he's now top of the A-list heap, and looks set to be there for a long, long time to come. 2010 looks set to be Zac's best year yet!

Home Sweet Home

No matter how big a star Zac has become, he has always managed to keep his feet firmly on the ground and never forgets where he came from. "Arroyo Grande is nice and warm," Zac says. "The perfect town for me to grow up in." It's clear to see that Zac's humble nature, honest values and strong personality come from his idyllic home town and solid family roots.

The Efrons are typical hardworking folk. His parents have been in love since the first day they met at the Arroyo Grande electrical plant, where they both worked in the early 80s. The angel of the family, Zac would spend his evenings and weekends studying for school and making sure his grades were always top-notch. Occasionally, he would be led astray by his cheeky brother, Dylan, who is four years his junior. While Zac is the

Zac **FACT**

Zac wasn't the first in his family to be involved in show business. His grandmother was in the circus!

artist of the family, Dylan likes to think of himself as the athlete, and is seriously into sports. Don't be surprised to see another famous Efron playing Major League Baseball in a few years! Growing up, Dylan was always causing trouble and loves pulling pranks on his superstar brother, especially when he gets too big for his boots. Zac is still super close to Dylan, who regularly hangs with his brother in LA where they still muck around and bug each other like crazy. "As my dad says, I love to stoop to his level," explains Zac. "We're just brothers. We goof off, and inevitably we fight; we have to fight it's in our blood."

Even though Dylan and the parents come to visit when Zac is in LA, Zac is often jetting around the world promoting his latest blockbuster flick. Zac would dearly love to spend more quality time with his family, in particular Dylan. "I wish I could say I spend more time with him," says Zac.

Some of Zac's favourite family memories are from when he, his brother and his dad would drive to the San Francisco Giants stadium to watch his sporting heroes play baseball. After the game the three boys would hang around the car park like groupies waiting to try to get a glimpse of their sporting heroes and possibly grab an autograph or two. So Zac knows what a thrill it is to get an autograph from one of his idols, which his why he always makes the best effort to try and sign as many autographs for his fans as he can.

Zac Quote

Zac on messing around with his bro: "Dylan made me reach into a dark scary hole to look for a golf ball he 'accidentally' threw in. When I put my hand down there, he screamed 'SNAAAAAKE!' at the top of his lungs. I almost passed out. He laughed."

Zac is a huge San Francisco Giants fan.

myzac factfile

Full name: Zachary David Alexander Efron

Nickname: Hollywood

Birthdate: 18th October 1987

Age: 22

Star sign: Libra

Home town: San Luis Obispo, California

Height: 5'9"

Parents: David and Starla

Siblings: One younger brother, Dylan

Pets: Two Australian Shepherds, Dreamer and Puppy, and a Siamese cat, Simon

About his pets: "My dogs are crazy. They're always getting into some kind of trouble ...but then again, they're my most loyal friends."

Favourite foods: Orange chicken from Panda Express, sushi, Wheat Thins, Japanese and exotic foods

Favourite cereals: Kashi, granola, Honey Nut Cheerios and Quaker Oats

Heaven on earth is: "Being first in line when the 'Krispy Kreme' employees hand out the free samples."

For dinner, Zac likes to make: "Mac 'n' Cheese! All the other stuff is too hard!"

Zac has a picture of Vanessa as the background on the screen of his iPhone.

most prized

His most prized possession: His autographed baseball collection: "I've got almost every player from the Giants for the past ten years."

First financial splurge: "I bought an electric scooter in sixth grade. It bankrupted me"

Before I die, I want to: "Discover I really do have super powers...I just didn't know it yet!"

People would be surprised that I: "Am just like they are."

Magazines Zac subscribes to: "*M&F, GQ, Cargo* and *Popstar!* Only because they have good posters of Jesse [McCartney]...Joke, dude!"

Boxers or briefs: Both!

Favourite actor/actress: Way too many to answer...

Favourite musician/band: Right now? Postal Service

favourite facts

Favourite movie: *The Goonies*, "hands down!"

Favourite music: Anything but country!

Favourite cartoon: *Rocko's Modern Life*

Favourite TV channel: Spike

Favourite TV show: *Most Extreme Elimination Challenge*, the *WSOP*, *American Idol* and *The Wiggles*

Favourite book: *Busting Vegas* by Ben Mezrich and *Robinson Crusoe* by Daniel Defoe

Favourite animal: Ligers (the lion and tiger mix-breed)

Favourite guilty pleasure: Comic books and video games

Role model: Peter Parker

Biggest fear: Zombies, sharks, the girl from *The Ring*

Favourite quote: "I'll be back" from *Terminator II*

Ticklish?: Yes!

Allergies: None!

On doing dares: "I'll eat just about anything – like blending up steak and apples, and then drinking it."

top talent

His hidden talent: "I can blow bubbles with my spit."

Weirdest dream: "I'm underwater and I can breathe and talk to fish and stuff. It was crazy."

On his driving test: "I cracked a cheesy joke and the instructor didn't laugh at all!"

Dream car: Toyota Supra from *The Fast and the Furious*

When I fly I have to have: "Rocket boots! Otherwise I always seem to fall."

What I'm reading: *Naruto*, Volume 7

The DVD release I was most excited about was: *Lords of Dogtown*

Zac **FACT**

- Zac's pearly-white teeth didn't get that perfect on their own – he had to wear invisible braces for six months to get them looking that good.

School Days

In the school halls, Zac wasn't quite the cool leader of the pack that we all know from *HSM* and *17 Again*. Because he was always running off to perform in the local theatre or TV shows, Zac was always playing catch-up, and could usually be found with his head in some books, making up time on the homework he'd missed because of his acting commitments. "I was always a sort of bookworm. I always tried to get the best grades, and I'm proud of that."

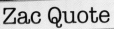

Zac Quote

Zac on teachers: "Teachers are people too. Get to know them. Well, don't 'suck up', but develop a relationship with each one individually. If you do a good job, the teachers feel morally obligated to give you every possible advantage in their class . . . Oh come on. Everyone knows it; I'm just saying it!"

According to Zac, his school, Arroyo Grande High, was just like *HSM*'s East High. "It was very similar [to East High],' says Zac, "only with less spontaneous singing and dancing."

Because Zac had a career in acting outside of school, he had a different perspective to most of the other kids and he always felt like an outsider. Rather than hanging with one particular group, he made sure always to hang out with everyone. Zac is a people person and likes to hang out with all sorts, from the nerds to the jocks. "In high school, I really didn't have a clique," Zac says. "I was more of a floater. I tried to hang out with everyone. I had friends in all groups."

Because of all his acting commitments during term, Zac always had to make sure he did his homework on time and never demanded special treatment from his teachers. When Zac graduated in 2006 he obtained a grade point average of 4.3, which is equivalent to an A+ in every subject. Looks, moves and brains! Zac's the complete package!

Hollywood Calling

Despite making an effort to move away from musicals of late, Zac's love of singing and dancing is a part of his soul, a fact that was obvious to his parents from an early age. When barely walking at just three years old, Zac was obsessed with musicals. Of course his favourites were old classics such as *The Wizard of Oz* and *The Jungle Book*. Zac would always sing along to the words of his favourite songs, and his parents noted how well he could sing. According to Zac, "When I was younger, my dad noticed that whatever song came on the radio, I would sing along to it and that I could carry a tune."

By the time he'd reached 11 years old, he was constantly sauntering around his house singing some happy tune. By this stage, it was more than clear to his parents that their boy had talent and they encouraged him to join the local theatre group. Of course he was terrified, like we all would be, at his first audition, but Zac's star quality was obvious to see for those sitting in the casting chairs and he landed his first part as the newsboy in his school production. Zac has never looked back. "From day one I got addicted to being on stage and getting applause and laughter." Zac loved the limelight and is still basking in it today.

It wasn't just his parents who could see what a superstar Zac was going to be. Even his teachers knew that he was destined for the bright lights of Hollywood. His drama teacher insisted on sending him to a talent agent that she knew in Los Angeles. Of course, his star quality shone through and the agency didn't need a second meeting to know that they had to sign up Zac before a competitor did. So far everything was falling so nicely into place for Zac, but he knew that hard work was ahead of him. He now needed to land his first television role.

Around this time in his life, Zac learned the importance of perseverance and patience. Poor old Zac and his dedicated mother used to have to drive all the way from Arroyo Grande down to Hollywood three times a week. Rarely was there a job at the end of the trip. Zac learned the meaning of rejection as he soon realised that Hollywood was a tough place to make a living, even for someone as talented as Zac! But Zac saw it all as a positive learning experience and trusted in his abilities, giving it his all at every audition.

Zac's faith and positive attitude proved strong enough to see him land his first TV role. Zac played the role of Simon (also the name of his Siamese cat) in an episode of *Firefly*, a futuristic sci-fi show for Fox. Once he broke the ice, the roles came thick and fast, with Zac appearing in shows such as *ER* and *CSI Miami*. The natural progression was to star in his first TV movie entitled *Miracle Run*. The industry was beginning to take note of the young stud and Zac was nominated for the Young Artists Award.

Zac Quote

Zac on auditioning: "You have to do your best every time, but after each audition you have to forget about it. You always have to be looking forward and not look back."

Zac on sharks: "In San Luis Obispo we've had a couple of shark sightings, but so what? Here's the thing – if a shark bites you, you are the luckiest dude in the world because you are a legend for ever."

Surfer Zac

Zac first became a pin-up poster boy when he landed the role of Cameron Bale in the hit teenage TV show, *Summerland*. He became an instant heart-throb in the US when he played Cameron the sultry surfer with a mysterious background. Zac says that "it was all about the drama. My character has some really deep and heavy issues. Luckily, I've never had to deal with the kind of intense pain he's had to deal with. That makes it really exciting for me." Originally only a short-term role, scripted in for two episodes, the producers and audience loved him so much that they made the role a full-time feature. Zac spent most of the time strutting around the beach in his boardies, and the lucky TV audiences got a first glimpse of his hot bod!

During the making of *Summerland*, Zac discovered a new passion… surfing. Playing the role of super-hunk surfer ignited Zac's love of riding gnarly waves. Ever supportive, his parents got him his first surfboard and wet suit the Christmas after he started filming the show. Out in the water, riding his first wave, Zac realised how tricky the sport was. "I got crushed by a wave and held under the water for about ten seconds. It was pretty scary." However, after a while he picked it up and is pretty good at it now. "I'm hitting the waves all over the place." Totally awesome, dude!

Cowboy Zac

Zac's meteoric rise was well underway by the time the Hollywood movie execs came knocking. *The Derby Stallion* was Zac's first big-screen production. However, just like learning to surf in *Summerland*, there was another skill required for his role: horse-riding. "I'd never done any horseback riding,' Zac says. "I assumed when I signed on for this movie that it was all going to be done by stuntmen. Then the first day when I came on set and talked to one of the producers, he said, 'Yes, you have three lessons and you're going to be jumping!' I guess that really turned on my adrenaline." Having never ridden a horse before, Zac jumped on and picked it up in no time. Zac soon learned to love the sport and still rides around the wilds of California today.

Zac Quote

Zac on his love of horse-riding: "It's a different experience and, at the same time, it's fun! It's so thrilling and amazing to be on top of a horse."

Zac Wordsearch

```
g  s  l  y  k  l  a  e  d  s
o  g  v  m  n  a  a  a  n  t
l  l  a  b  t  e  k  s  a  b
r  a  t  i  u  g  v  a  l  a
a  s  u  r  f  b  o  a  e  d
l  s  k  y  d  i  v  e  r  s
i  e  h  g  n  i  v  l  m  r
b  n  l  l  a  t  r  o  s  m
r  a  v  e  g  r  o  t  u  o
a  v  l  a  r  y  y  i  s  u
```

troy
basketball
summerland
surfboard
vanessa
guitar
libra
ashley
skydive

Answers on pg 62

Zac Crossword

Answers on pg 62

ACROSS

3. The name of Zac's cat
6. Zac's nickname
7. Zac's gorgeous girlfriend
8. Zac's favourite city
9. The first concert Zac ever went to

DOWN

1. Zac's star sign
2. Zac's favourite animal
4. Zac's favourite band
5. The family member who was in the circus

HIGH SCHOOL MUSICAL

When Disney announced that they were holding auditions for a new teen flick entitled *High School Musical*, budding young stars flocked from all across the US to the Disney studios. The cast began to take shape as Corbin Bleu, Vanessa Hudgens and Ashley Tisdale all wowed the casting directors with their talents. However, right up until the final day of casting, the producers still hadn't found an actor to play the lead role of Troy Bolton.

On the last day of their long search for talent, the Disney producers were frustrated at not having found the perfect guy to play the lead role. Just before they were about to call it a day and go home, Zac strutted through the audition room doors and blew them all away with his effortless cool and charming persona. Troy Bolton had arrived. When asked to sing and dance in front of a room full of strangers, Zac found it all came easily: "I had it easier than some guys at the *HSM* audition – some of them were passing out! It was Broadway-style, seven and a half hours of dancing, singing and acting."

Zac **FACT**

With the popularity of *High School Musical*, Zac had to change his phone number after getting numerous calls from fans.

Preparing for the role was intense. None of the young cast was that experienced and they had to learn all the songs and dance moves in a matter of weeks, which put them all under extreme pressure. "We didn't know what we were doing; we were thrown into this dance room and there were mirrors everywhere! We didn't know anything about each other and had to learn these dances. We had two weeks of intense dancing, acting, singing and basketball rehearsals, along with strange stretching exercises and things I'd never heard of before. We'd wake up at six in the morning and work until six at night. I learned more in those two weeks than I'd learned in all the previous years." The hard work paid off for Zac, Vanessa, Ashley, Corbin, Monique and Lucas, and the evidence is there for all to see in the three spectacular movies.

Zac Mania

No less than 7.7 million of us huddled around our TV sets to watch the first screening of *High School Musical*, obliterating every single one of Disney's previous viewing records. From the first screening there was no looking back and boys and girls across the world were singing and dancing to *We're All In This Together* and *Get'Cha Head in the Game*.

But how similar are Zac and Troy? Ever humble, Zac is always extremely modest when comparing himself to the prom king, Troy. Deep down he knows his similarities to the character make him the only person who could play Troy: "I was sort of in the same boat as Troy when I was hanging out at school. Everyone thought it was so cool to be part of the basketball team, but to go out and be in plays at the local theatre houses wasn't that cool, I guess."

And what is the secret to *HSM*'s success? "Girls love the romance and boys love the whole basketball and sports angle of the show." Almost overnight, *HSM* mania spread across the globe, and with that every girl in the world's knees became weak at the sight of Zac.

Soon enough *High School Musical 2* and *3* came out and Zac's popularity went nova. The summer of 2007 became known as "The Summer of Zac" and the boy wonder became the hottest thing since Brad Pitt. Inevitably, the big-time movie offers came streaming in. Despite all the new superstardom, Zac's favourite part of making *HSM 2* and *3* was getting together with all the old gang again: "It was great to be with all the guys again. It was fun. Like a reunion."

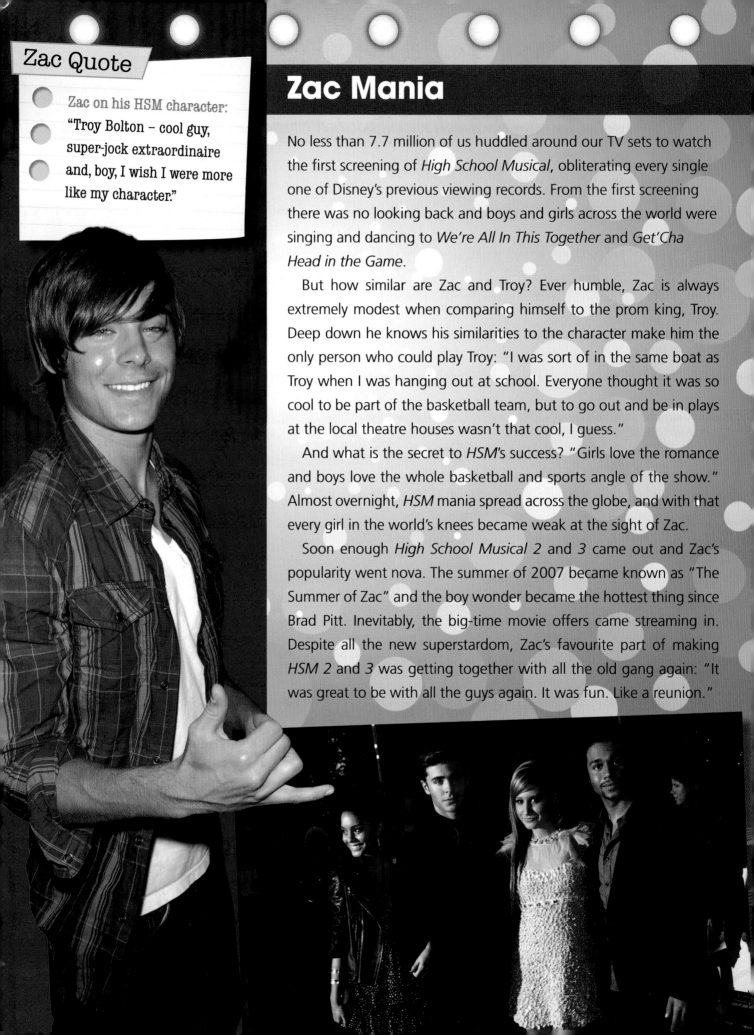

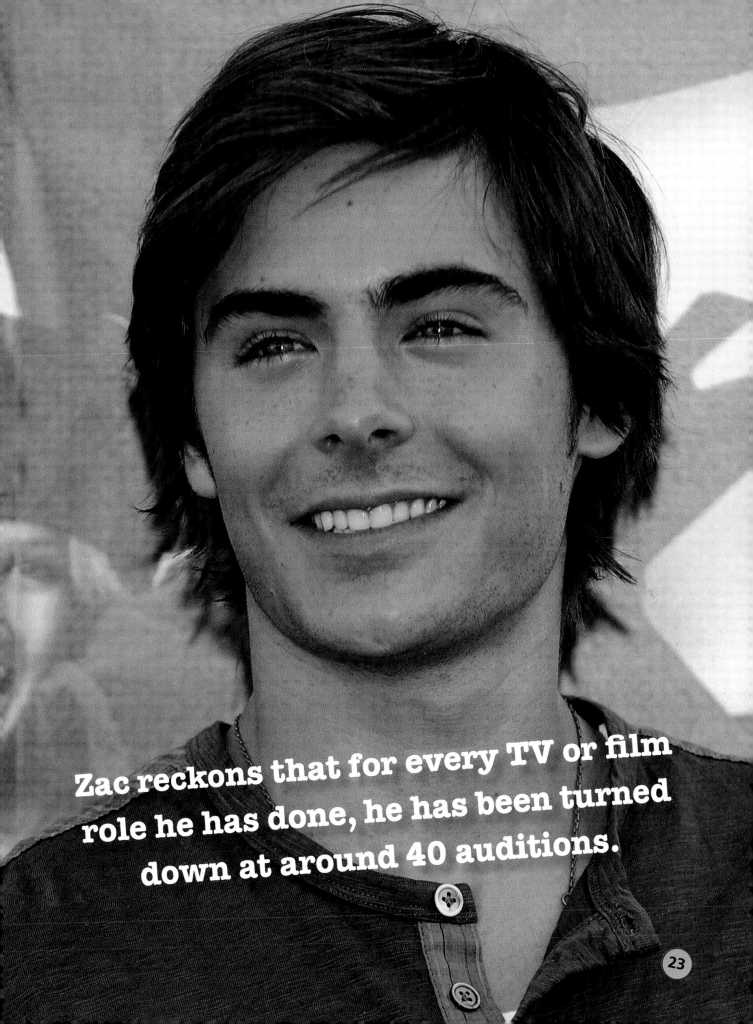

Zac reckons that for every TV or film role he has done, he has been turned down at around 40 auditions.

Make Your Own Charm Bracelet!

With exquisite taste in everything from how he styles his hair to what clothes he wears, Zac definitely has an eye for those who are as stylish as he is! So here is a guide to keep up with the trends by making your own trendy charm bracelet!

1. The String

First off, you'll need to find yourself some ribbon or coloured wool. Once you have, cut it into a length that, when tied, will fit snugly – but not too tightly – around your wrist. You can even double the thickness or plait it into a lovely strand if you would like to put some heavier charms on it.

2. Decorating

Now it's time to jazz up your bracelet! Get any beads or small jewels you can find and attach them to your bracelet either by putting the string through the middle or using extra bits of string to tie them on. You can use any favourite small items, from earrings to rings that don't fit, right through to phone charms! Hey, it's recycling too.

24

Remember, the colour of the string is important – picking one that fits your personality will go a long way to showing what kind of girl you are. Here is some advice as to what colours go with what sort of personality:

Red
Girls who wear red are often passionate and full of energy. It is a colour that shows you have courage and you will often enjoy energetic activities such as sports and games.

Orange
This normally means that you are enthusiastic and happy. You enjoy giving encouragement to others, live a healthy life and are very creative.

Yellow
The colour of sunshine means joy and happiness. Wear yellow and you cheer everyone around you and grab attention from others.

Green
Girls who like green will probably also like nature. You like to be safe and have a stable life, while you are also very hopeful.

Blue
This is the colour that that means you are wise and loyal, other people can trust you and you aren't shallow. Another important thing about blue is that it's one of the favourite colours for boys!

Purple
When most people think of purple they think of royalty. Wear purple and you are powerful, noble, ambitious and enjoy luxurious things. If you plan on wearing it try to use a light purple as a darker shade can mean you are sad and gloomy!

White
Girls in white are innocent and pure; this is also seen as the colour of perfection. You are effortlessly cool and have a lot of faith in other people.

Black
The colour of power and elegance shows you are a handful! It shows other people you are mysterious and unknown, but also very strong and have a lot of depth.

Final Touches

It's a good idea that your outfit and nails match the jewellery, but if they don't that's OK because a charm bracelet is meant to be worn all the time – you never know when you'll have the chance to talk about it to some great guy who's asking about your amazing jewellery. It's like your personality is around your wrist! Go crazy and put as many different charms on there as you like.

THE BIG TIME

Almost direct from *HSM*, Zac sung and danced his way on to the set of *Hairspray*, another musical which he shot with Christopher Walken, Queen Latifah and his hero and idol, John Travolta, who played the role of Tracy Turnblad's mother. To work with such a huge superstar, on whom Zac had modelled his career, was mind-blowing for Zac. "When I met John, I was speechless. Everything that John Travolta has done, I'd like to do in the future."

Zac's performance as the slick 60s kid Link Larkin reminded many people of Travolta's performance as Danny Zuko in *Grease*, and it's no surprise that Zac is now great friends with his mentor and colleague, Travolta.

17 Again

The 2009 release of *17 Again* saw Zac play the teenage version of *Friends* star Matthew Perry. In it Zac plays the role of the teenage Mike O'Donnell, who as an adult – played by Matthew Perry – gets the chance to turn into a kid again and change his life. The film is Zac's first lead in this type of film and if the success of last summer's movie is anything to go by, we can expect plenty more in the future. According to Zac he still gets lots of offers to do musicals but he's keen try out different stuff and increase his versatility as an actor, rather than stay in his comfort zone. "Everything else that was around was either a musical or a high-school romance, you know, and this was actually the biggest risk and the biggest challenge," Zac says. "I can relate to playing a kid – I've had a first kiss, I've had awkward dates, I've had fights with my parents...But one thing I've never done is gotten into a fight with my teenage daughter."

Zac Quote

Zac on being a 36-year-old in a 17-year-old's body: "It was interesting. I've always been kind of an old man, so to speak."

Zac FACT

If Zac could have one super power it would be to know what people are really thinking.

29

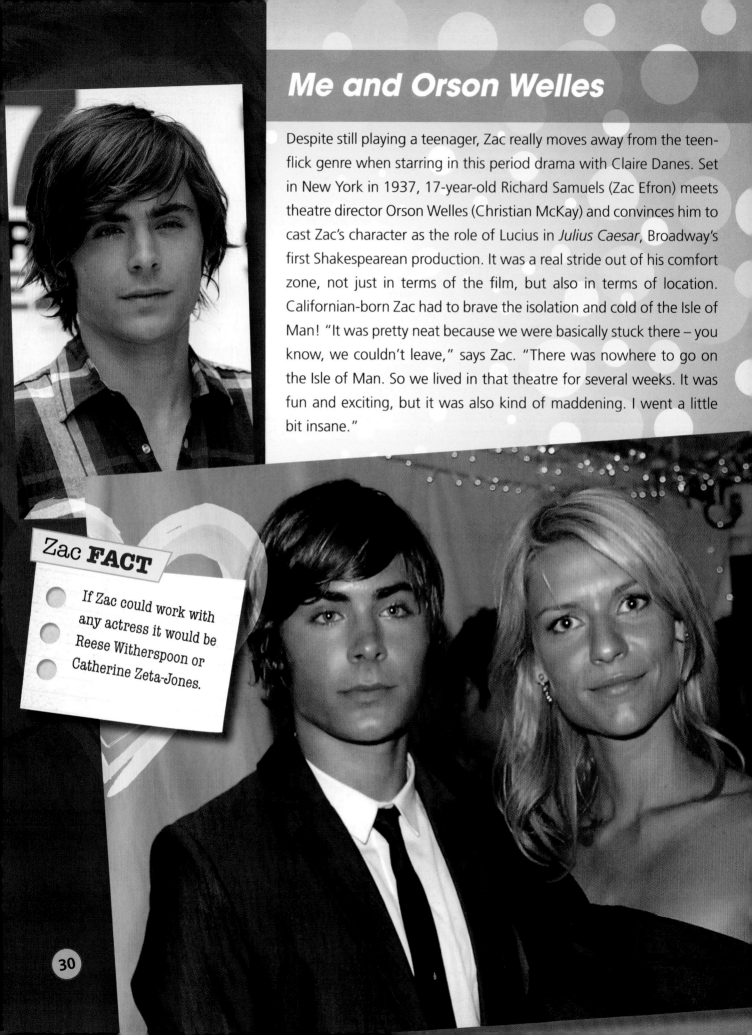

Me and Orson Welles

Despite still playing a teenager, Zac really moves away from the teen-flick genre when starring in this period drama with Claire Danes. Set in New York in 1937, 17-year-old Richard Samuels (Zac Efron) meets theatre director Orson Welles (Christian McKay) and convinces him to cast Zac's character as the role of Lucius in *Julius Caesar*, Broadway's first Shakespearean production. It was a real stride out of his comfort zone, not just in terms of the film, but also in terms of location. Californian-born Zac had to brave the isolation and cold of the Isle of Man! "It was pretty neat because we were basically stuck there – you know, we couldn't leave," says Zac. "There was nowhere to go on the Isle of Man. So we lived in that theatre for several weeks. It was fun and exciting, but it was also kind of maddening. I went a little bit insane."

Zac FACT

If Zac could work with any actress it would be Reese Witherspoon or Catherine Zeta-Jones.

Hollywood Mentors

Since being elevated from teen star to A-list Hollywood actor, Zac has been hanging with all kinds of big-time celebs. His new Tinsletown pals who've been helping Zac in his fledgling career include…

Claire Danes

Claire's a lucky girl, not only did she get to play the star-crossed lover opposite super hunk Leonardo DiCaprio in *Romeo & Juliet*, she now gets to play Zac's seductress in his first serious big-screen production, *Me and Orson Welles*. Just like Zac, Claire's career began with singing and dancing in stage musicals. Only rather than having a sunny West Coast Californian upbringing like Zac, Claire was raised in the hustle and bustle of New York. Claire and Zac became friends when they starred in *Me and Orson Welles*, and spent large parts of 2008 promoting their joint project, including a trip together to the Toronto Film Festival for the premiere of the film. The two have plenty in common, with Claire having been a huge teen star in the TV series *My So-Called Life*. They also both love to sing and dance and spent much of their time together talking about their favourite musicals. Having starred in major Hollywood blockbusters such as *The Hours* and *Terminator 3,* Claire understands what it takes to make the elevation from teen star to serious Hollywood actor, and is a guiding influence on Zac during this transitional period of his career. Just like a big sister!

Claire on...

Fame: "I think people confuse fame with validation or love. But fame is not the reward. The reward is getting fulfilment out of doing the thing you love."

Her idol: "Madonna was my original muse – around five-years-old, I saw her perform on TV, and I realised that performing could be one's vocation."

Going to college while being an actress: "I was told that my going to college wouldn't be good for my career. I think that's nonsense. It's good to empower yourself by cutting yourself off from this business every once in a while."

Being a child star: "I'm only realising now that I was a child actress because I always took myself so seriously."

David Beckham

Fame: "The spotlight will always be on me, but it's something I'm learning to live with as the years go by."

An alternative career: "I always wanted to be a hairdresser."

Hobbies: "Shopping, I've got more clothes than Victoria."

Becks and Zac have met at many Hollywood parties and the gorgeous pair have since become good friends, with David becoming a bit of style guru for Zac: "I love the way he dresses," says Zac. David and Zac both understand what it's like to deal with fame at an early age. Becks was thrust into the limelight as a teenager, and was the pin-up poster boy of his generation, just like Zac. David understands how to deal with constant media attention while maintaining high standards in his professional life and Zac admires that. Even though David is spending more time in Milan these days, his family still live in Los Angeles and the two get to catch up whenever he's in town.

One day Zac hopes that he and Vanessa will be as revered as Posh and Becks: "Vanessa and I would love to be like the US David and Victoria Beckham. It's funny when we're compared to them, I just can't believe it."

Zac FACT

Zac attended the World Cup in Germany with Corbin Bleu.

Zac Quote

Zac on Leo and their friendship: "He's smart, level-headed, charming, hilarious. You know, the older-brother vibe. That sounds so cheesy."

Leo on...

The secret of success: "If you can do what you do best and be happy, you're further along in life than most people."

Fame: "All I see is more people looking at me than before. But, you know, who cares? You just can't obsess yourself with this fame stuff."

Acting: "Don't think for a moment that I'm really like any of the characters I play. That's why it's called acting."

Dating: "My first date was with a girl named Cessi. We'd had a beautiful relationship over the phone all summer long. Then she came home and we met to go out for the first time to the movies. When I saw her I was petrified. I couldn't even look her in the eye to talk to her."

Leonardo DiCaprio

Leo has become like the big brother Zac never had. The pair hang out at LA Lakers basketball games together, and Leonardo passes on advice about how to make it from a teen idol to a respected Hollywood icon, just like he did. His main message to Zac? Stay away from drugs, of course. Leo told Zac, "If you really want to mess this all up, try heroin. Seriously, that's pretty much the only way you're going to screw this up, and you shouldn't go down that road – it will mess you up without fail. Do not do drugs." Obviously Zac isn't that silly, but with Leo by his side he's sure to have just as long and successful career as his pal. The crazy thing is, when Zac was a young teenager he was envious of Leo: "When *Titanic* came out, all the girls would go crazy over him, so you kind of hated the guy," says Zac of his buddy. Look who all the girls are going crazy over now, Zac.

Being a comedian: "After I got my first laugh on stage, I was hooked."

His *Friends* character, Chandler: "The guy everybody thinks will do well with women, but he thinks too much and says the wrong thing."

Asking out Julia Roberts: "I was like: I'm going to ask Julia Roberts out but I'm going to be very nervous about it. Then she said yes, and I got even more nervous."

Dating: "I've learned the key to a good date is to pay attention to her."

Zac FACT

In Ashton Kutcher's MTV show Punk'd, Ashton pranks Zac when he is accused of helping a thief steal some money from a Rodeo Drive boutique. Guess who was behind the prank? Zac's friend Ashley, of course.

Matt Perry

In *17 Again* Zac became good friends with *Friends* actor and co-star Matt Perry. Known to most of us as the joker Chandler, Matt plays the 36-year-old version of Zac in the film. In order to study for the role, Zac says, "I didn't have to sit down and watch seasons of *Friends*, I was already familiar with the show. Just hanging out with Matt was the most valuable thing. He was always available to help me and we became friends making the film."

In turn Matt was impressed by how dedicated and hardworking Zac was, saying that "Zac would call me on my cell to ask how I'd deliver lines and say certain things, which is a testament to how cool a guy he is." After working with Matt, Zac is now keen to move on to more comedies in the future, leaving his musical past behind him. You never know, Zac may even get involved in a sit-com like Matt: "I think Matt's doing pretty well, so I'd love to be like him," says Zac.

John Travolta

One of Zac's personal career highlights to date has been getting the chance to work with his hero, John Travolta. According to Zac, the first time he had to do a scene with the *Grease* and *Saturday Night Fever* star, "I was shaking in my boots. I was star-struck. To be honest, I'm just glad I got through it." To date Zac has modelled his career on John's, and just like John some 30-odd years ago, he's going to make the step away from musicals and into more mainstream cinema. Who better to guide him through the transition than the great John Travolta? Ever since he wowed audiences as the all-singing, all-dancing hunk, Danny Zuko, Travolta has gone on to be one of the most respected actors in Hollywood, starring in films such as *Look Who's Talking* and *Pulp Fiction*.

John on...

Loving airplanes: "I called my son Jett and I wanted to call my daughter Qantas but my wife wouldn't let me."

His role as Edna in Hairspray: "It was tough dancing in high heels, but we did change the heels to more of a dance shoe – like a Capezio. You know they kept giving me these skinny high heels and it's like, 'OK, I understand those. My mother wore those.'"

On dancing on Broadway: "It's a tough rite of passage. I did 13 years of it. Summer theatre, off-Broadway, Broadway, and whoa, enough is enough, it's a lot of work, eight shows a week for a year or two at a time. But yes, I think it's a certain rite of passage."

Make Your Own "I ♥ ZAC" T-Shirt!

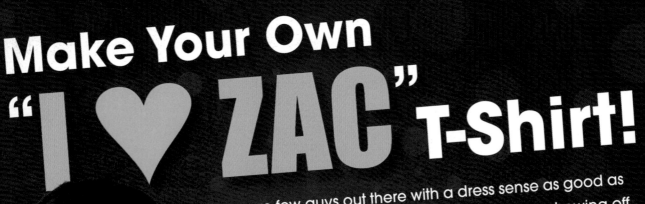

There are few guys out there with a dress sense as good as Zac's. Try designing your own piece of clothing, showing off your love for all things Zac, and it might be the stepping stone to making something so cool even Mr Efron himself would wear it!

What you will need to get started...

- A plain white T or an old T-shirt with or without sleeves
- Some fabric crayons, pens or paint
- Fabric glue (optional)
- Sequins and stick-on jewels (optional)
- A pencil and rubber

Where to begin...

Start off with your basic design. You can use a soft pencil for this as it will wash out later, so don't worry if you want to change your design. So how about writing "I LOVE ZAC" on the T-shirt in a crazy style? You could use any kind of size letters but think about how the T-shirt will be worn...perhaps you could even work the design right around the shirt?!

Now that you've got started, here's how to give it some added Zac magic...

○ Add glitter to the letters or just in random patterns to give it that extra sparkle.

○ Think about the colours, do you want it one colour and then add lots of detail? Or do you want it to be jazzy and multi-coloured?

○ A cool slogan draws attention to a T-shirt. It could be something about Zac, or just one of your favourite catchphrases.

○ How do you want the T-shirt shaped? Short-sleeved or long-sleeved? Baggy or figure-hugging? Plenty of accessories attached, or nice and simple? These all affect how your T-shirt will turn out.

Now is the time to draw the design that you have in your head on to the T-shirt. Remember that it's important to have a plan of your design before you start drawing:

Are you happy with it? Would you wear it yourself? If you want to make your design a reality you could give it a go by buying a plain white T-shirt and using paints and glitter to bring your ideas to life!

myzac quizfile

myzac quizfile 1–9

1. **If Zac could swap lives with one person, who would it be?**
   a) The Pope
   b) Brad Pitt
   c) The Queen
   d) Barack Obama

2. **What does Zac say his dream job would be?**
   a) professional surfer
   b) testing video games
   c) chocolate taster
   d) astronaut

3. **What was Zac's favourite television show?**
   a) *Batman*
   b) *Power Rangers*
   c) *Hannah Montana*
   d) *Teenage Mutant Ninja Turtles*

4. **Who is the most famous person Zac has the number of in his mobile phone?**
   a) The President of China
   b) Tom Cruise
   c) Prince William
   d) Ian McKellen

5. **Which supermodel did Zac used to have a poster of on his wall when he was younger?**
   a) Tyra Banks
   b) Kate Moss
   c) Lindsay Lohan
   d) Naomi Campbell

6. **What is the first thing Zac notices in a girl?**
   a) voice
   b) smile
   c) smell
   d) eyes

7. **Which type of music is the only one Zac doesn't listen to?**
   a) hip-hop
   b) country
   c) classical
   d) jazz

8. **Which instrument did Zac teach himself to play?**
   a) drums
   b) harp
   c) guitar
   d) violin

9. **In the first *High School Musical* movie, how many songs did Zac sing in?**
   a) 4
   b) 7
   c) 5
   d) 10

quizfile 10–13

10. **What was the name of the first television series Zac made a guest appearance on?**
    a) *Firefly*
    b) *Firefox*
    c) *Firehydrant*
    d) *Fireinthedisco*

11. **Zac appeared in a music video for a Hope Partlow song in 2005, what was the name of the song?**
    a) "Sick Outside"
    b) "Guilty Inside"
    c) "Bad Feelings"
    d) "Sick Inside"

12. **What was the name of the character played in an episode of *The Suite Life of Zack and Cody*?**
    a) Benjamin
    b) Trevor
    c) Walter
    d) William

13. **What does Zac, so he can have privacy, do in the mornings when nobody else is doing it?**
    a) go out for dinner
    b) go to the cinema
    c) buy clothes
    d) go dancing

myzac quizfile 14–20

14. When he is warming up his voice, what word does he sing in different notes?
a) bumblebee
b) cheese
c) Vanessa
d) posy

15. What can't Zac stand being around?
a) bad dancers
b) poor dressers
c) funny voices
d) smokers

16. Which of these items of clothing does Zac love to wear?
a) hoodies
b) sandals
c) baseball caps
d) waistcoats

17. What does Zac enjoy making for dinner the most?
a) tuna salad
b) lasagne
c) macaroni and cheese
d) hamburger

18. In his movie *17 Again*, Zac plays an older man who has been transformed back into a 17-year-old, but which actor played the older version of Zac?
a) The Rock
b) Leonardo DiCaprio
c) Matthew Perry
d) Prince Charles

19. Zac's girlfriend and fellow *High School Musical* star Vanessa Hudgens released her own album in 2007. What was the name of the music video in which Zac appeared?
a) "Say No"
b) "Say Maybe"
c) "Say OK"
d) "Say For Sure"

20. Which one of these men does Zac consider to be his acting idol?
a) Johnny Depp
b) Christian Bale
c) Robert Pattinson
d) George Clooney

Zac sang "Let Me Love You" by R&B star Mario in his first singing audition.

answers

20) a- Johnny Depp
19) c- "Say OK"
18) c- Matthew Perry
17) c- macaroni and cheese
16) b- sandals
15) d- smokers
14) a- bumblebee
13) b- go to the cinema
12) b- Trevor
11) d- "Sick Inside"
10) a- *Firefly*
9) c- 5
8) c- guitar
7) b- country
6) d- eyes
5) a- Tyra Banks
4) d- Ian McKellen
3) d- *Teenage Mutant Ninja Turtles*
2) b- testing video games
1) c- The Queen

Love Life

Young Love

Zac had his first kiss when he was 13: "It was in a game of truth or dare. I can picture her face exactly! I can't believe I can't think of her name." No doubt she remembers his name. Ever since high school Zac has had girls throwing themselves at him. Even in class he'd have notes passed to him from wannabe girlfriends: "When I was in first grade, this girl passed me a note in class that said, "Do you like me?" and there was a box that said, "check yes, or check no." I checked yes and handed it back to her. It was really funny, romantic awesomeness." But despite moving on to great levels of stardom, Zac is still in contact with first girlfriend: "My first crush and I are still friends to this day. We text message and call each other all the time."

Zac's Kissing Do's and Don'ts

The first kiss is a big deal – ask Troy and Gabriella. Zac gives his definitive guide to kissing. Take note...

Do
"Go easy and take your time. Be respectful of the other person and don't just get on in there and grope all over the place. My favourite kisses happen when I've taken it nice and slow."

Don't
"Try to swallow the person you're kissing by opening your mouth so wide! I've never experienced a washing-machine kiss, but I've heard about them. When girls rotate their tongues around your mouth like a washing machine, that's not a good idea."

What Zac Looks For in a Girl

How many of Zac's top-ten criteria do you tick?

To be one of Zac's girls it helps if…

☑ ☒

1 You have brown hair. While Zac loves a bubbly blonde, his real soft spot is for brunettes.

2 You've got a good singing voice. Zac loves to sing when pottering around the house, and likes to have a girl he can do duets with.

3 You possess a generous heart. Zac can't stand mean-spirited people, and loves kind folk, like him.

4 You like to talk: "I think if a girl is easy to talk to then that's the first thing I look for," says Zac. "It's great when you meet a girl and three hours later you're like, 'Oh my gosh, we've been talking for three hours, what happened to the time?' I just think that is a great connection and you know there is potential there."

5 You have soulful eyes (preferably brown). Zac is a sensitive guy and needs to be able to look deep into a girl's eyes.

6 You don't get jealous. Zac sees jealousy as a weak personality trait, and will often have to work with other pretty girls, so he needs his girlfriend to trust him.

7 You look curvy. Nothing is less attractive to Zac than skinny, size zero models: "I like my girls like I like my peanut butter, chunky."

8 You smell sweet. Zac loves nothing more on a girl than the smell of "a good perfume. I like the smell of Pink Sugar."

9 You like Japanese food. He loves going for sushi on dates.

10 You don't hum. It's one of Zac's greatest pet peeves. Zac's worst ever date was with a girl who hummed. According to Zac it was "so annoying".

Zac on Dating

"Ask out your crushes. And when you do, you'll be so happy you did it. You've got to put yourself out there, because if you do you'll have no regrets. The worst thing to do is stew on the perfect way to approach a girl. If you do that, then you think about it too much and you're bound to mess it up. If you just go out there and start giving hints and being yourself around the girl, hopefully she'll return some of the vibe and you guys will click. I'll start up a conversation and not lead on at all that I like them. I get them talking and if they talk back, and we eventually find a connection…And if we don't, it's over."

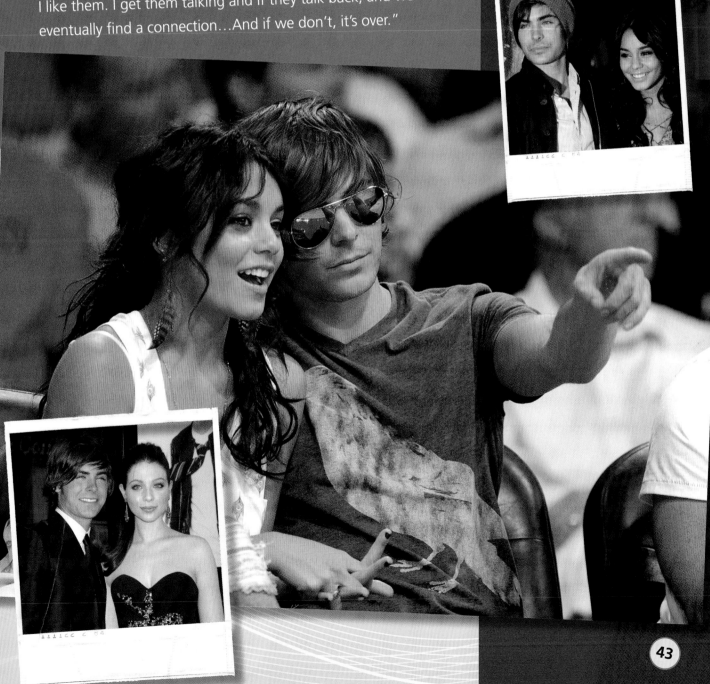

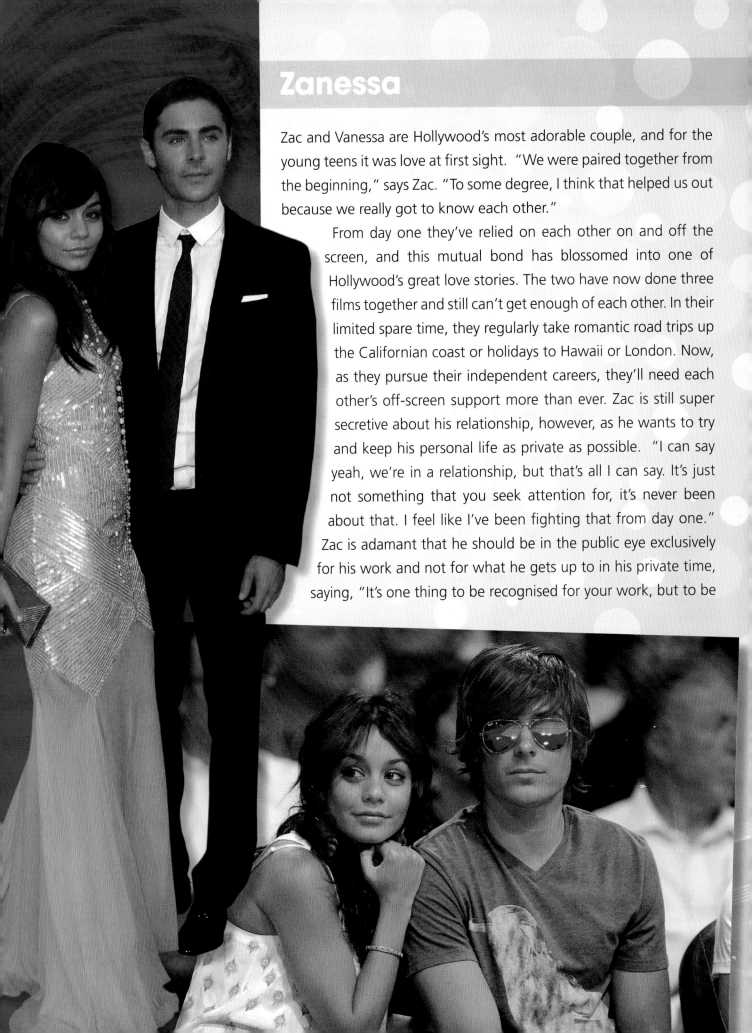

Zanessa

Zac and Vanessa are Hollywood's most adorable couple, and for the young teens it was love at first sight. "We were paired together from the beginning," says Zac. "To some degree, I think that helped us out because we really got to know each other."

From day one they've relied on each other on and off the screen, and this mutual bond has blossomed into one of Hollywood's great love stories. The two have now done three films together and still can't get enough of each other. In their limited spare time, they regularly take romantic road trips up the Californian coast or holidays to Hawaii or London. Now, as they pursue their independent careers, they'll need each other's off-screen support more than ever. Zac is still super secretive about his relationship, however, as he wants to try and keep his personal life as private as possible. "I can say yeah, we're in a relationship, but that's all I can say. It's just not something that you seek attention for, it's never been about that. I feel like I've been fighting that from day one." Zac is adamant that he should be in the public eye exclusively for his work and not for what he gets up to in his private time, saying, "It's one thing to be recognised for your work, but to be

Ten Reasons Why Zanessa Are Destined To Be Together

Zac and Vanessa's many similarities...

1. They're both from California.

2. They both started acting as children and were teen stars that liked to act, sing and dance.

3. Before *HSM*, the two independently guest starred on *The Suite Life of Zack and Cody* with Ashley Tisdale, whom they both consider to be one of their closest friends.

4. The dream couple are both desperate to go skydiving one day.

5. In their most recent films before *High School Musical 3*, they both worked with *Friends* stars. Zac co-starred alongside Matthew Perry, and Vanessa with Lisa Kudrow.

6. They love kangaroos.

7. Peter Pan is one of their favourite children's stories.

8. They both hate smoking.

9. Their favorite city is London.

10. They're both gorgeous!

Zac FACT

Zac's duet with Vanessa, "Breaking Free", made the fastest climb in American chart history – climbing from number 86 to 4 in only 14 days.

recognised for your personal life, it's not admirable, I've never been interested in that."

But will we be hearing wedding bells and seeing baby Zanessas soon? "Right now? No. Right now there's no more terrifying prospect than raising a family, I'm far too selfish at the moment," says Zac. "I don't think I'm responsible enough, so I think that's years and years down the road."

Design Zac's New Hairdo!

Even though Zac's haircut is pretty close to perfection, why don't you try and see if you can find a style that might suit him better! You may prefer him with shorter or longer hair, or even with it a different colour! And there's only one way to find out!

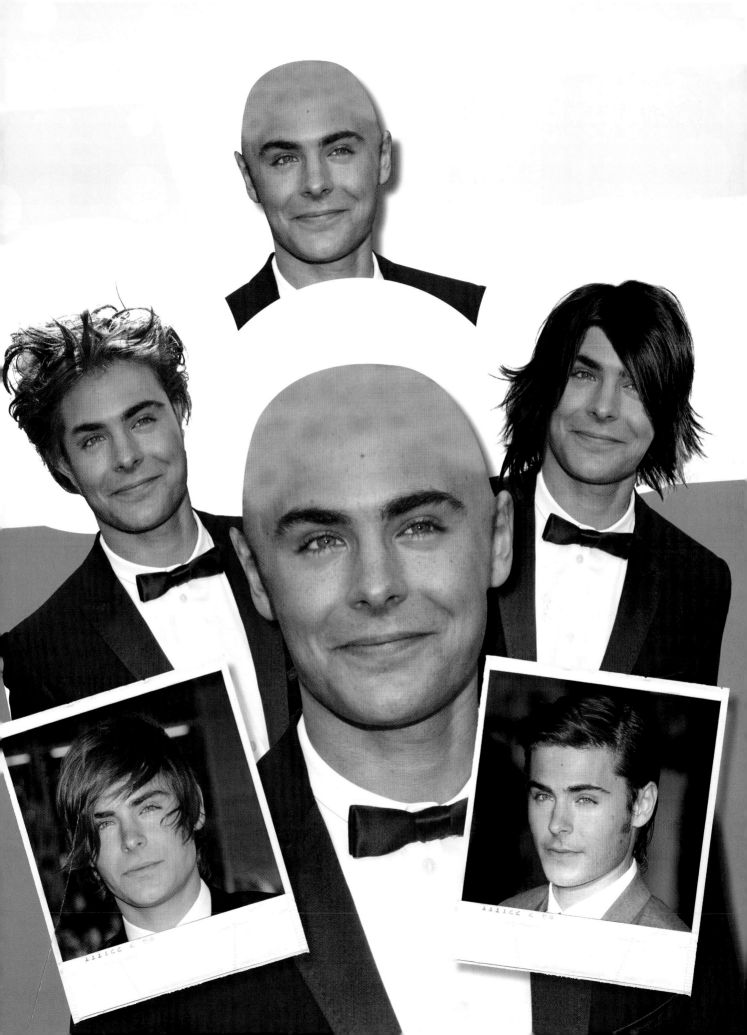

Interests and Hobbies

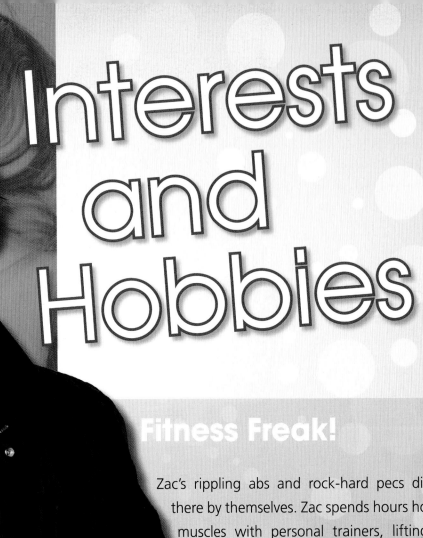

Fitness Freak!

Zac's rippling abs and rock-hard pecs didn't just get there by themselves. Zac spends hours honing his sexy muscles with personal trainers, lifting dumb-bells and sweating it out on rowing machines. His super-healthy lifestyle means he wakes most mornings and goes for a run along Manhattan Beach although he says "it's getting harder to go to the beach these days as so many people recognise me." He'll then grab a health shake and hit the weights with his brother Dylan. "After watching the entire *Rocky* series, I got hooked on fitness," says Zac. He now has the *Rocky* theme tune as the ringtone on his mobile phone.

Zac FACT

Zac's most prized possession is his autographed baseball collection.

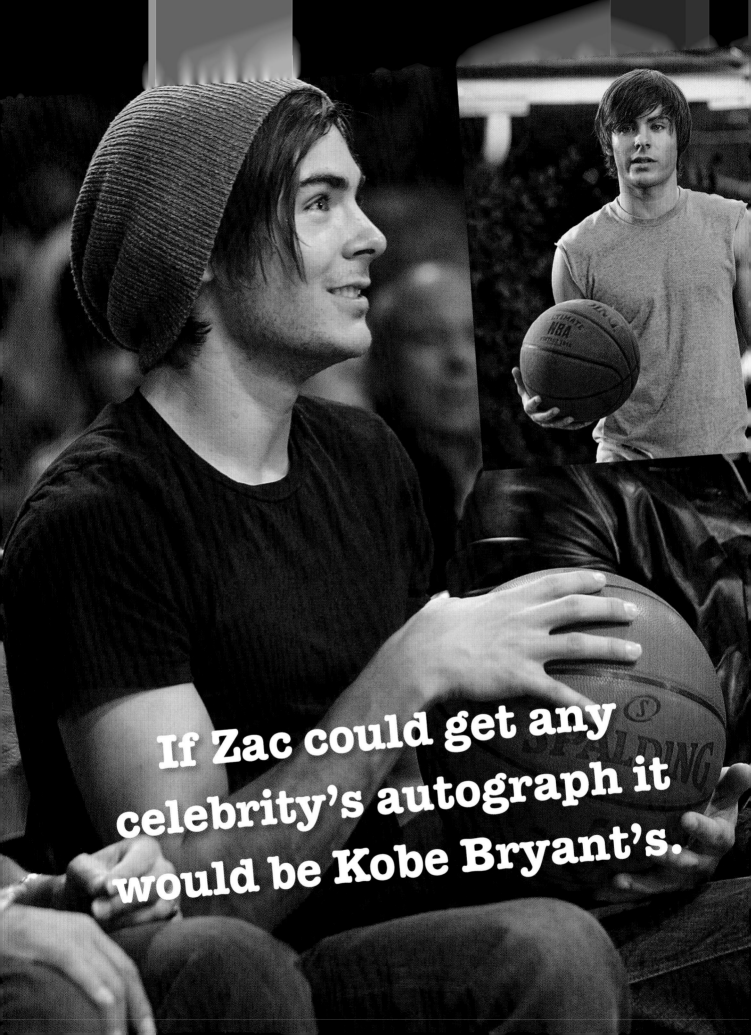

If Zac could get any celebrity's autograph it would be Kobe Bryant's.

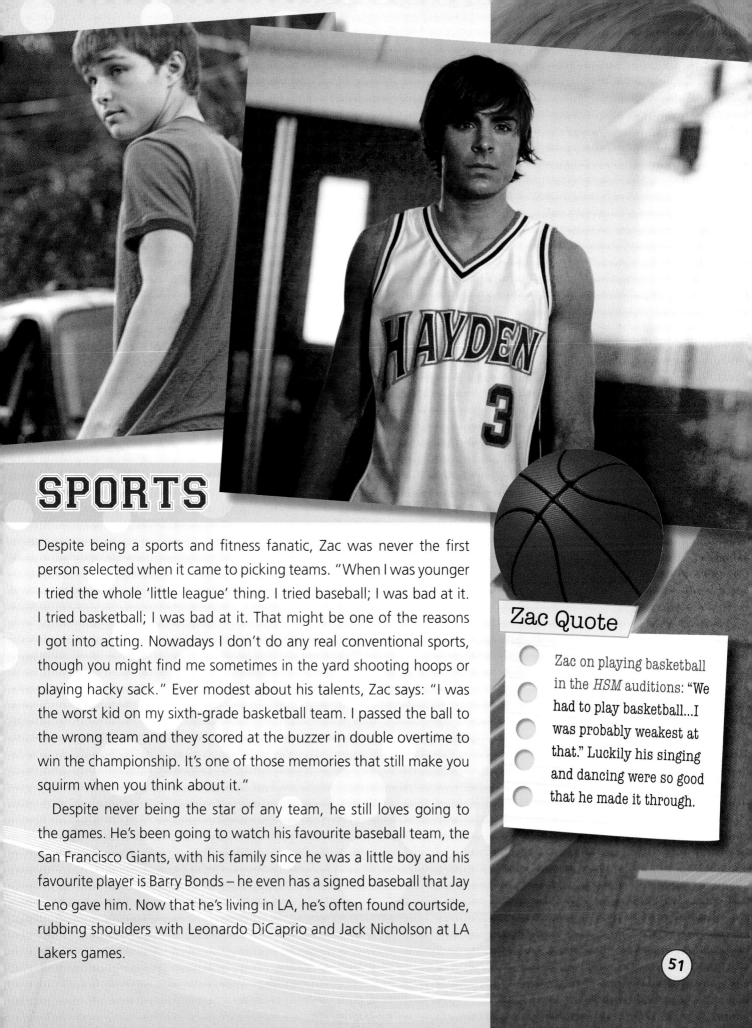

SPORTS

Despite being a sports and fitness fanatic, Zac was never the first person selected when it came to picking teams. "When I was younger I tried the whole 'little league' thing. I tried baseball; I was bad at it. I tried basketball; I was bad at it. That might be one of the reasons I got into acting. Nowadays I don't do any real conventional sports, though you might find me sometimes in the yard shooting hoops or playing hacky sack." Ever modest about his talents, Zac says: "I was the worst kid on my sixth-grade basketball team. I passed the ball to the wrong team and they scored at the buzzer in double overtime to win the championship. It's one of those memories that still make you squirm when you think about it."

Despite never being the star of any team, he still loves going to the games. He's been going to watch his favourite baseball team, the San Francisco Giants, with his family since he was a little boy and his favourite player is Barry Bonds – he even has a signed baseball that Jay Leno gave him. Now that he's living in LA, he's often found courtside, rubbing shoulders with Leonardo DiCaprio and Jack Nicholson at LA Lakers games.

Zac Quote

Zac on playing basketball in the *HSM* auditions: "We had to play basketball...I was probably weakest at that." Luckily his singing and dancing were so good that he made it through.

Adrenaline Junkie!

As a kid he was always into adrenaline sports like skiing, snowboarding and rock climbing, but his main passion was skateboarding. He says, "One day I'd love to do a skydive. I'm definitely going to do it in the next year." Also, just like Troy in *HSM 2*, Zac is a keen golfer and often makes it out to LA's courses for a swift 18-holes. His acting career has introduced him to a few new sports. Ever since filming *The Derby Stallion* he's had an interest in horses, and loves to take a steed out for a gallop along the Malibu beaches whenever he gets a chance. Also, *Summerland* got him hooked on surfing, something he still loves doing today. But at heart Zac is still a skater boy. "I've always loved skateboarding. The way you glide is almost Zen."

Zac **FACT**

Zac is currently fixing up an old DeLorean (the car from *Back to the Future*) left to him by his grandfather.

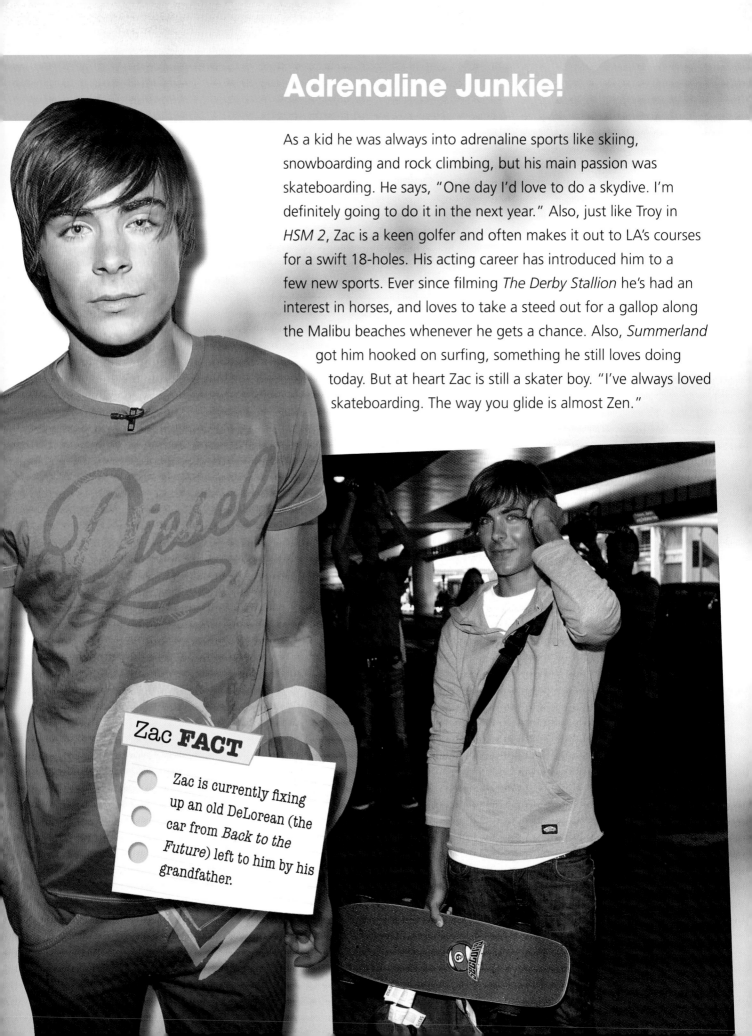

Music

Although he's making an effort to move away from musicals lately, Zac will always love singing. "I've always been singing. Since day one," says Zac. But despite having chart-topping success with "Get'Cha Head in the Game" and "Breaking Free", Zac is keen to focus on acting, for now. "I'm going to work primarily on the acting, to try to make a foundation for myself for the future...I'm definitely just an actor." Even big-money deals from the likes of Simon Cowell (of *X Factor* fame) have been turned down in favour of concentrating on his acting. "I'm trying to steer clear of the whole music thing at this point. I think the most important thing is to establish myself as an actor. I think it's very easy for people to start getting confused when they see a CD come out."

So we could be waiting a while before Zac follows his fellow *HSM* cast members and releases an album. However, wherever Zac goes his ipod is never too far away: "I'm into anything and everything. I'll just go on to iTunes and download hundreds of stuff."

Zac's Favourite Album Releases in 2009

U2 – *No Line on the Horizon*

Ben Harper & Relentless 7 – *White Lies For Dark Times*

Green Day – *21st Century Breakdown*

Black Eyed Peas – *The E.N.D.*

Moby – *Wait For Me*

Looking at the Stars for 2010

Zac's Astrology

As a Libra, Zac is excellent in friendships and partnerships, a great friend and a great co-star. He is great to work with, hang out with or date – if you are lucky enough. He's a true boyfriend who is honest and trustworthy, what more could you want? Dazzling blue eyes perhaps? Check! Got those too…

But no one is perfect – or are they? Zac has been known to find it hard to make decisions and is sometimes afraid of choosing the wrong path; he's sometimes torn between singing and dancing but hey, when you are great at both it must be hard. But as he has shown in 2009 he's moving on from the dancing and is acting his way into our hearts. So with his artistic loves you can't blame a guy for being good at everything, so perhaps he is perfect after all!

Zac dressed up as a dustbin last Halloween.

57

2010 ZAC LIKES

- getting notes and e-mails
- being pampered
- foreign travel
- fans!

2010 ZAC DISLIKES

- shouting
- sloppiness
- dirty places
- criticism

What do the stars say?

We know if he met you he'd fall in love with you, but which star sign is Zac most compatible with?

You're the one!

Aquarius – a marvellous match

Gemini – sublime

Aries – opposites attract

Scorpio – emotionally rewarding

Taurus – very sensual

Sorry, there's a Zac clash...

Capricorn – don't bet on this one

Cancer – very hard work

Virgo – you'll disagree

Libra – indecisive!

Sagittarius (Vanessa Hudgens) – too flighty

Other famous Librans include Gwen Stefani, John Lennon, Matt Damon, Sting, Mahatma Ghandi, Avril Lavigne, NSync's Chris Kirkpatrick and Gwyneth Paltrow.

ZAC'S 2010 OUTLOOK

Family

Zac has been so busy this year he really has missed his family – even his brother's prankish style! 2010 will be a time for some home cooking and catching up with the gang.

Love

Romance is looking hot in 2010. Zanessa is looking as strong as ever and Zac has the love and support he has always dreamed of. But hey, he hasn't met you yet, so who knows!

Friendship

Being on set makes it hard to keep up with friendships but Zac is a very special guy and takes his closest pals and their problems seriously. As his schedule gets busier and he's off around the world on another film tour, we see a BIG mobile phone bill in his future. Hey, it's worth it!

Career

Zac has made the big leap from *HSM* to other hit movies in 2009. And as he goes from strength to strength in 2010, all of his fans will be watching him closely. The roles he considers and then accepts are going to be more serious in 2010, but he will keep us constantly entertained and wow us with his hidden, and not so hidden, talents.

If Zac wasn't an actor he'd be a college student.

Looking to the Future...

Now that Zac has officially decided to move on from musicals, we can be sure that Zac won't be starring in *High School Musical 4* or anything else, for that matter, that involves him singing and dancing in 2010. What we can expect is to see Zac take a new direction as he aims to gain the respect of the industry as a serious actor. As the man says himself, "It's time to take a new direction."

○ Zac has donated many
items to Rocky Stone
to be given to less
fortunate kids as part
of the Toy Mountain
Campaign.

Zac **FACT**

○ Zac's favourite city?
London!

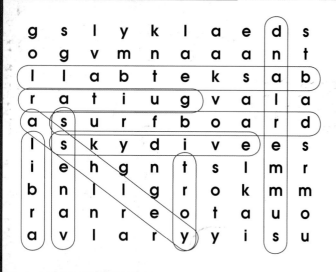

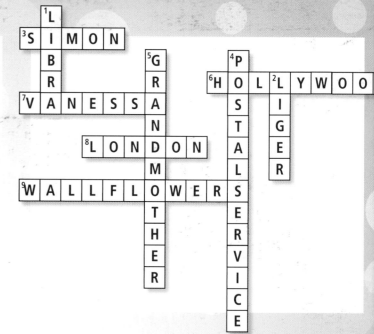

Picture Credits

Getty: 2, 4, 5, 7, 9 (top left), 12 (bottom right), 15, 17, 20, 21 (top right), 22 (bottom right), 23, 24 (centre), 30, 31, 32, 33, 34, 35, 36, 38, 39, 40 (centre left and bottom left), 41, 43 (top right), 44 (left), 46 (bottom right), 47 (centre), 48, 50 (centre), 52 (bottom right), 53, 54, 56, 58, 63

Rex: 9 (centre right), 11, 12 (top left), 13 (top), 19, 21 (centre right), 28, 29, 37, 46 (bottom left), 49, 50 (top right), 51, 52 (centre left), 55, 57, 59, 60, 61

PA Photos: 6, 8, 10, 16, 22 (left), 27, 40 (bottom right), 43 (centre and bottom left), 44 (bottom), 45, 46 (centre right), 47 (bottom left and bottom right)

Corbis: 14, 26

iStockphoto: 24 (centre right)

Acknowledgements

Posy Edwards would like to thank Helia Phoenix, Amanda Harris, Jane Sturrock Helen Ewing, Tim Edwards, James Martindale and Rich Carr.

Copyright © Posy Edwards 2009

The right of Posy Edwards to be identified as the author of this work has been asserted in accordance with the Copyright, Designs and Patents Act 1988.

First published in hardback in Great Britain in 2009 by Orion Books an imprint of the Orion Publishing Group Ltd Orion House, 5 Upper St Martin's Lane, London WC2H 9EA An Hachette Livre UK Company

1 3 5 7 9 10 8 6 4 2

A CIP catalogue record for this book is available from the British Library.

ISBN: 978 1 4091 1330 0

Designed by www.carrstudio.co.uk
Printed in Italy by Rotolito Lomardo

The Orion Publishing Group's policy is to use papers that are natural, renewable and re-cyclable and made from wood grown in sustainable forests. The logging and manufacturing processes are expected to conform to the environmental regulations of the country of origin.

Every effort has been made to fulfil requirements with regard to reproducing copyright material. The author and publisher will be glad to rectify any omissions at the earliest opportunity.

www.orionbooks.co.uk